HAUNTED WORLD

A SPINE-TINGLING TOUR OF THE WORLD'S
MOST HAUNTED PLACES

AMBER BULLIS, MATT CHANDLER, AND **JILLIAN HARVEY**

CAPSTONE PRESS
a capstone imprint

Haunted World is published by Capstone Press,
1710 Roe Crest Drive, North Mankato, Minnesota 56003
www.capstonepub.com

Library of Congress Cataloging-in-Publication Data
Cataloging-in-publication information is on file with the Library of Congress.
ISBN 978-1-4966-2125-2 (paperback)

Editorial Credits
Carrie Braulick Sheely, editor; Kyle Grenz, designer; Svetlana Zhurkin, media researcher; Kathy McColley, production specialist

Photo Credits
Alamy: Antony Souter, 11, davidwallphoto, 16, Karina Tkach, 88-89, Radius Images, 30-31, Víctor Suárez, 21; AP Images: Dylan Lovan, 71, Patron Spirits/Greg Wahl-Stephens, 79; Bridgeman Images: Private Collection/Portrait Miniature of Lady Anne Barnard (w/c on ivory in gilt-metal frame), Mee, Anne (Mrs Joseph) (c. 1760-1851)/Photo © Philip Mould Ltd, London, 17; Courtesy of the Federal Bureau of Investigations: 91; Dreamstime: Arik Chan, 54-55, Jackbluee, 72, Kaido Rummel, 5 Background, Lesapi, 14, Ruud Glasbergen, 65 Left, 75, Sue Martin, 99, 101; Getty Images: Hindustan Times/Prasad Gori, 42, Marco Di Lauro, 110, Paris Match/Manuel Litran, 121, The LIFE Picture Collection/Pictures Inc./ Time Life Pictures, 107, The Montifraulo Collection, 40-41, UIG/Wild Horizons, 82-83; iStockphoto: duncan1890, 116, Goddard_Photography, 13, Philartphace, 119, simongurney, 62, spanglish, 65 Right, 74; Library of Congress: 27 Bottom, 90-91; Matt Chandler: 84; Newscom: akg-images/A.F. Kersting, 106, Danita Delimont Photography/Walter Bibikow, 80, Dumont Bildar/picture-alliance/Arthur F. Selbach, 23, Heritage Images/The Print Collector, 115, Heritage Images/Werner Forman Archive/Euan Wingfield, 32, Kyodo, 61, NI Syndication/Gill Allen, 113, Pictures From History, 56, Sipa USA/Sipa Asia/Yu Yi, 48, Westend61 GmbH/Harald Nachtmann, 102-103, Zuma Press/Donal Husni, 50-51; North Wind Picture Archives: 76; Shutterstock: Ad_hominem, 93, Design Element, Aleksey Stemmer, 104-105, alredosaz, 118, Amir Bajrich, 70, Anton Belo, 27 Top, Arina P Habich, 35 Background, Armita, 33, Design Element, Azman AlKurauwi, 44-45, Benny Marty, 92, Benoit Daoust, 111, Brian Kinney, 28, Chepe Nicoli, 81, chloe7992, 85, David Steele, 8, Daxiao Productions, 5 Front, dikobraziy, 63, Design Element, Dmitry Tereshchenko, 95 Front, Elenarts, 19, EQRoy, 60, Fer Gregory, Cover Top Right, GolubaPhoto, 43, Guillermo Pis Gonzalez, 95 Background, HandmadePictures, 9, Joe Prachatree, 35 Front, 65 Middle, Kush Rathod, 38, Mahod84, 57, Marcos Carvalho, 77, MartinMojzis, 87, michaeljung, 22, MM Stock, 69, Mohd Nasri Bin Mohd Zain, 53, Nanisimova, 108, observe.co, 120, Olga_i, 117 Top, paula french, 114, Peter Etchells, 122, Peter Titmuss, 15, photo.ua, 78, PrakichTreetasayuth, 12, Pyty, 123, Design Element, Scharfsinn, 109, Sergii Rudiuk, 58-59, Songkran Wannatat, 117 Bottom, Songquan Deng, Cover Middle, Sopotnicki, 24-25, Stas Guk, 98, Waj, 29, windsketch, 68, zef art, 6, 36, 66, 96, 128; Wikimedia: ChingMing, 39, Daniel Case, 47

Printed and bound in China.
1732

HAUNTED WORLD

FAMOUS GHOST STORIES OF AFRICA

E STRUGGLE FOR FREEDOM AND

TABLE OF CONTENTS

Scary Ghost Stories of Africa

What was the last ghost story you heard? Maybe it involved a local **haunted** cemetery or hotel. People tell similar spooky tales all over the world. Some of these stories come from Africa. Does a ghostly woman join party guests at a historic castle in South Africa? Do ancient Egyptian kings haunt their burial places? Decide for yourself as you explore some of Africa's most haunted places.

haunted—having mysterious events happen often, possibly due to visits from ghosts

Tokai Manor House In Cape Town, South Africa, is said to be haunted by a ghostly horse and rider.

Simon's Town

LOCATION: CAPE TOWN, SOUTH AFRICA

For more than 200 years, Simon's Town has been a Navy base for the South African Navy. Today the base is known not only for its military importance but also for its ghost stories. Spooky stories about Simon's Town include ghosts who bang on doors and knock paintings from walls. Some people have felt unexplained chilly air in hallways. In one building witnesses have reported the ghosts of a nurse and an old man who sits on a toilet.

Magistrates used a building called The Residency in the early 1800s. The Residency was home to cells where guards chained and punished prisoners. Today locals say the ghosts of former prisoners haunt The Residency. Some visitors claim to have seen ghost prisoners in a cell. Unexplained chilly winds blast through the rooms and cell doors bang shut on their own. Some people believe one of the ghosts is a seaman who faced a gruesome death. A guard's wife who treated prisoners poorly is also said to haunt the building.

In 1982, The Residency became the Simon's Town Museum. Workers at the museum have reported seeing a ghost in old-fashioned clothes. They say she turns off lights, moves objects around, and makes noises in empty rooms. Workers began to call her the "Grey Lady" because she is often seen wearing a grey dress. One story says she is the ghost of a servant who lived at The Residency in the 1700s. She was in love with a sailor but was not allowed to see him. Another story says she is the ghost of a teenage girl who once lived at The Residency.

magistrate—a government official who makes and enforces laws

Simon's Town Museum

Soweto Ghost Child

LOCATION: JOHANNESBURG, SOUTH AFRICA

On June 16, 1976, schoolchildren protested in the Soweto neighborhood in Johannesburg, South Africa. During the protests, 13-year-old Hector Pieterson was shot by police. A reporter took his picture as the injured boy was carried away. Hector died from his wounds. A South African newspaper published the picture, and other newspapers around the world soon did too. It was one of the most important moments in the struggle against apartheid in South Africa. It showed the world what was happening there. It led to continued protests against apartheid, which would later be known as the Soweto Uprising.

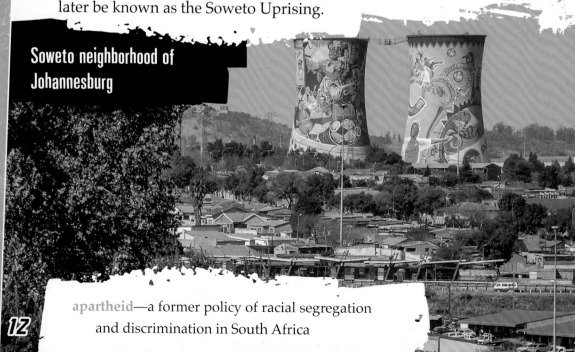

Soweto neighborhood of Johannesburg

apartheid—a former policy of racial segregation and discrimination in South Africa

Today there is a memorial to Hector and others who died in the uprising near where he was shot. At the foot of the hill after sunset, people claim to see Hector. He has his fist raised in a black power salute. Some people say the faint sound of gunfire can also be heard.

FACT

South Africa made June 16 a holiday. People remember the 1976 protest on this day.

The Castle of Good Hope

LOCATION: CAPE TOWN, SOUTH AFRICA

The Dutch East India Company built the Castle of Good Hope between 1666 and 1679. The trading company wanted the fort to provide protection in case the settlement was attacked. The castle is the oldest building still used today in South Africa. Some believe it's also the most haunted. In the late 1600s, locals used the Castle of Good Hope for fancy balls, ceremonies, and other events. But the castle also had a dark side. An underground prison and torture chamber called the "dark hole" was deep within its concrete walls. Officials imprisoned, tortured, and executed people held in the dark hole. Could the castle's bloody past explain some of its paranormal events?

execute—to put to death

paranormal—having to do with an event that has no scientific explanation

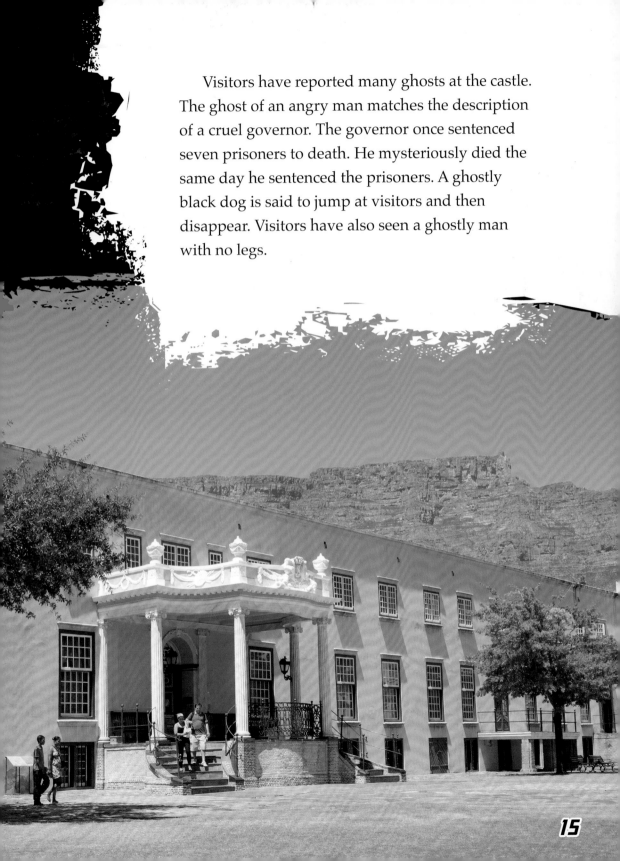

Visitors have reported many ghosts at the castle. The ghost of an angry man matches the description of a cruel governor. The governor once sentenced seven prisoners to death. He mysteriously died the same day he sentenced the prisoners. A ghostly black dog is said to jump at visitors and then disappear. Visitors have also seen a ghostly man with no legs.

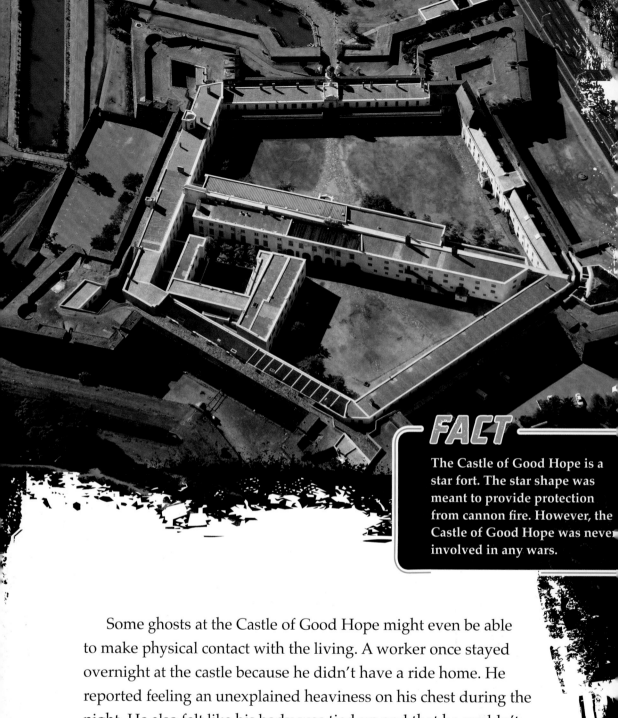

Some ghosts at the Castle of Good Hope might even be able to make physical contact with the living. A worker once stayed overnight at the castle because he didn't have a ride home. He reported feeling an unexplained heaviness on his chest during the night. He also felt like his body was tied up and that he couldn't move. After struggling free, he ran out of the room, terrified.

One of the most famous ghosts of the castle
is said to be of Lady Anne Barnard. Lady Anne
moved with her husband, Andrew Barnard, to
the Castle of Good Hope in 1797. She hosted
grand parties there. Castle guards have reported
seeing Lady Anne's ghost in a beautiful gown
joining guests at ballroom parties.
A painting of peacocks that Lady Anne
hung is still on a wall in her
former drawing room. It is
said that anyone who
moves it will die.
Castle workers now
keep it covered
just to be safe.

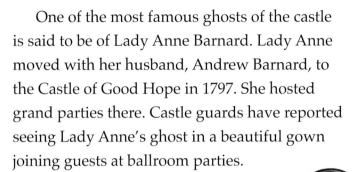

**Lady Anne
Barnard**

The Flying Dutchman

LOCATION: SEA SURROUNDING THE CAPE OF GOOD HOPE, SOUTH AFRICA

The *Flying Dutchman* is one of the most famous ghost ships of all time. In 1680, Captain Hendrick Van der Decken and his crew set sail from Amsterdam on The *Flying Dutchman*. The ship was carrying expensive goods. As the ship sailed by the Cape of Good Hope, stormy weather caused high waves. The ship sank and the crew drowned.

Since The *Flying Dutchman* sank, sailors have reported seeing the ghost ship. Many of these sightings happen during bad weather. Some stories say The *Flying Dutchman* approached other ships until they almost collided before the ghost ship disappeared. Other stories say the ghost ship sent an eerie glow into the sky or appeared in the middle of a red flame. The most famous person to see the ghost ship is said to be King George V of England. Before becoming king, he served in the Royal Navy. In 1881, he was aboard the ship *Bacchante*. He wrote about the crew's ghostly encounter with The *Flying Dutchman* in his diary.

Sailors aren't the only ones who say The *Flying Dutchman* still haunts the waters around the cape. On at least two separate occasions, crowds at a beach saw The *Flying Dutchman*. The ghost ship is said to have disappeared after almost colliding with the shore.

FACT

It's said that a sailor who sees *The Flying Dutchman* will die shortly afterward.

Sarpan Island

LOCATION: DAKAR, SENEGAL

Just off the coast of Dakar, Senegal, is tiny Sarpan Island. It's one of the rocky islands of the Iles de Madeleine and is part of a national park. According to legend, it is also home to a magical **spirit** called a genie, or djinn.

Local fishers believe the genie protects them. But if someone makes the genie angry, the genie will keep that person from catching any fish. Some even say it will crash the offender's boat on the rocks of the island. According to a guide, the captain of a Spanish tuna boat saw a light on the island in 2013. The boat ran aground. However, no one lives on the island and there are no lights.

The genie does not want anyone living on the island. In the 1700s, a man named Lacombe tried to build a house there out of island rock. According to legend, the spirit kept destroying the house. He later left the island with the house unfinished. Visitors can still see the ruins today.

spirit—an invisible part of a being that contains thoughts and feelings; some people believe the spirit leaves the body after death

FACT

Sarpan Island is known for its small baobab trees and the seabirds that nest there.

Port Elizabeth Public Library

LOCATION: PORT ELIZABETH, SOUTH AFRICA

Some people call the Port Elizabeth Public Library the most beautiful building in South Africa. In 1902, builders constructed the library with gorgeous archways, stained-glass windows, spiral staircases, and a large glass dome. Yet its impressive appearance may be hiding some spooky secrets.

Locals say the library has been home to at least two ghosts. Before the library's construction, a different building stood on the library grounds. In 1896, a fire destroyed it. When firefighters tried to put out the fire, a large piece of stone fell off the building and killed a police officer. Locals put up a stone to remember the policeman. As construction of the new library began, workers moved the stone to the garden. But the police officer's ghost might not have been happy about the new location of his remembrance stone. People say he haunted room 700 of the library until workers moved the stone back to its original location.

People believe a former library caretaker also haunts the building. Robert Thomas worked at the library for 31 years. Since his death in 1943, workers say doors mysteriously open and shut and books move or fall when no one is around. Could Thomas's devotion to the library have kept him there even after death?

Menengai Crater

LOCATION: NAKURU, KENYA

The mysterious Menengai Crater is located about 100 miles (160 kilometers) from Nairobi, Kenya. It's the crater of a volcano that erupted thousands of years ago. Hot vents in some parts of the crater still give off steam today.

The name *Menengai* seems to have come from the Maasai culture. It means "place of the dead." In the 1800s, two groups of Maasai fought each other at the crater. According to legend, the winners threw the losers into the crater.

FACT

The Menengai Crater is the second largest volcanic crater in the world.

Locals sometimes call it "Devil's Place," for the **supernatural** beings said to live there. These beings are even said to farm on the crater floor. The crops would be planted, grown, and harvested within a day. Some people think the spirits trick visitors and hunters into getting lost. Sometimes they disappear. Other times they are found wandering after several days. When asked, they can't seem to explain how they got lost.

supernatural—something that cannot be given an ordinary explanation

Valley of the Kings

LOCATION: LUXOR, EGYPT

Ancient Egyptians used the Valley of the Kings as a burial site from about 1539 to 1075 BC. Egyptians buried pharaohs and other royal leaders in the tombs. They mummified the bodies to preserve them for the afterlife. With all the dead bodies there, it may not be surprising that the site has been the focus of some creepy ghost stories.

The valley is one of Egypt's major tourist sites. Some visitors have reported unexplained feelings of being watched. Others report hearing ghostly screams and mysterious footsteps. The most common ghost story tells of a pharaoh wearing a golden headdress. He haunts the valley on a chariot pulled by black ghost horses.

Visitors to the valley also have reported seeing the ghost of the pharaoh Akhenaten. Egyptian priests are said to have put a curse on him because he banned worship of the Egyptian gods. The curse forced him to wander the valley forever. Could the curse have worked?

afterlife—the life that some people believe begins when a person dies

mummify—to preserve a body with special salts and cloth to make it last for a very long time; the preserved bodies are called mummies

pharaoh—a king of ancient Egypt

The Mummy's Curse

Some people believe anyone who disturbs the body of an ancient Egyptian pharaoh will come under "The Mummy's Curse" or "The Curse of the Pharaohs." It is said to cause sickness or even death. The curse became popular after Howard Carter and his crew discovered King Tut's tomb in the Valley of the Kings in the early 1920s. Some of the men who found the king's tomb suddenly died not long after the tomb was opened. Today researchers believe their deaths can be explained in other ways. But some still believe in the power of the curse.

Howard Carter (left) and an assistant with King Tut's coffin

The Pyramids of Giza

LOCATION: GIZA, EGYPT

Egyptians used the Pyramids of Giza as tombs for pharaohs before the Valley of the Kings. They built the Pyramids of Giza between about 2575 and 2465 BC. Three pyramids make up the landmark. Pharaoh Khufu ordered the building of the biggest pyramid, known as the Great Pyramid. Ancient Egyptians built the second pyramid that includes the Sphinx for pharaoh Khafre. The Sphinx is a statue with the body of a lion and the head of a pharaoh. Pharaoh Menkaure ordered the third and smallest pyramid.

People reported ghosts at the Pyramids of Giza as early as 1900. Witnesses have reported seeing the ghost of a British soldier with fiery eyes. The soldier is said to have fallen from one of the pyramids in 1882. Another ghost haunting the area is said to be of a worker who died running machinery nearby.

Dr. Paul Brunton spent the night in the Great Pyramid in the 1930s. He said he felt his entire body go numb and cold. He saw ghostly figures move across the room. One raised its hands and came at him in a threatening way. Does something paranormal go on at night in the pyramids? Few people get permission to stay there overnight, so perhaps we'll never know.

FACT

Archaeologists are still unsure how ancient Egyptians built the massive pyramids at Giza. Scientists say the pharaohs needed between 20,000 and 30,000 workers to build the Great Pyramid. These workers had to transport about 2.3 million stone blocks that each weighed 2.5 to 15 tons (2.3 to 13.6 metric tons)!

Kaf Ajnoun

LOCATION: NEAR GHAT, LIBYA

A natural rock formation in Libya called
Kaf Ajnoun has many names, and most of them
relate to ghosts. It is known as the Mountain of Ghosts, the
Devil's Hill, and the Fortress of Ghosts. The local Tuareg
people believe spirits live there. Many locals are so scared of
the spirits that they will not travel near it.

The Tuaregs share stories of wicked spirits that gather on the mountain and will scare anyone who tries to climb it. In the 1500s, a traveler wrote that evil spirits haunted the mountain. He said spirits confused travelers so they couldn't find their way home. Explorers who have dared to go there have often encountered difficulties. Two different explorers in the mid-1800s got lost on the mountain and nearly died. One was the famous explorer Heinrich Barth. He ran out of water and survived by drinking his own blood.

Some locals believe the ghosts that live on the formation can even enter the bodies of animals and people. One story tells of evil spirits entering wasps to warn climbers to stay off the mountain. French travelers who wanted to hike the mountain raced back to their vehicle after a swarm of wasps attacked them, leaving their faces full of painful stings. They never climbed the mountain. In 2004, explorer Kira Salak climbed the mountain. At first, she believed she made it home safe. But months later, she said evil ghosts entered her body. Could the local stories be true? Explorers may want to stay far away from Kaf Ajnoun so they don't find out.

FACT

One man said he watched an army of terrifying ghosts marching on the mountain before they suddenly disappeared.

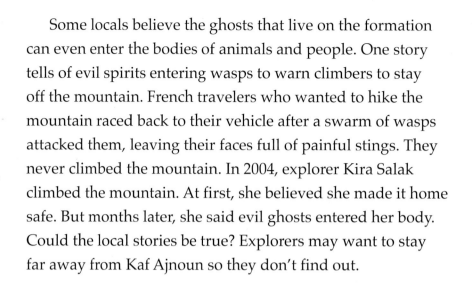

Camels help Tuaregs travel around the hot African deserts.

Haunted Locations of Africa

1. Simon's Town, South Africa
2. Soweto Ghost Child, Johannesburg, South Africa
3. The Castle of Good Hope, Cape Town, South Africa
4. *The Flying Dutchman*, seas near Cape of Good Hope
5. Sarpan Island, Dakar, Senegal
6. Port Elizabeth Library, Port Elizabeth, South Africa
7. Menengai Crater, Nakuru, Kenya
8. Valley of the Kings, Luxor, Egypt
9. The Pyramids of Giza, Giza, Egypt
10. Kaf Ajnoun, near Ghat, Libya
11. Rudd House, Kimberley, South Africa
12. Kempton Park Hospital, Kempton Park, South Africa

FAMOUS GHOST STORIES OF ASIA

TABLE OF CONTENTS

Spine-Tingling Ghost Tales

Ghost stories come from every corner of the globe. Asia is the world's largest continent, and it is rich with haunted places. Looking for creepy graveyards? Want to hear about piercing shrieks in the night coming from **abandoned** buildings? You can find them in Asia. No one knows if ghosts are real. But one thing is certain: These ghostly tales from Asia will send a tingle up your spine!

abandoned—deserted or no longer used

Bhangarh Fort is known as one of the most haunted places in India.

2 High Street

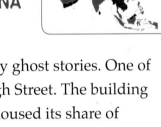

LOCATION: HONG KONG, CHINA

Hong Kong, China, is home to many ghost stories. One of its most haunted places stands at 2 High Street. The building is more than 125 years old, and it has housed its share of dreadful events. Some people believe these events led to the reports of hauntings.

British nurses first lived at 2 High Street after it was built in 1892. These nurses worked at a nearby hospital. During World War II (1939–1945) the building became a **psychiatric** hospital. Female patients with mental disabilities lived there. In 1961, a competing hospital opened, and 10 years later the hospital at 2 High Street shut its doors. For nearly 30 years no one lived in the building. But was it really empty?

psychiatric—related to a branch of medicine that studies the mind, emotions, and behavior

Soon after it closed, people started reporting ghostly sightings at 2 High Street. Some people said headless **poltergeists** wandered the halls at night. People heard unexplained screams echoing from within the walls. The building's best-known tale is of a ghostly figure dressed in traditional Chinese clothing. If it meets eyes with the living, it bursts into flames.

the hospital at 2 High Street in 1900

poltergeist—a noisy ghost

In 1998, workers built the Sai Ying Pun Community Center at 2 High Street. The L-shaped front of the old building remains. Today the center is bustling with visitors all day. But the building's ghost stories are alive and well. Once the sun sets, only the brave dare step inside.

FACT

After it was abandoned, the old hospital at 2 High Street became known as the "High Street Haunted House."

Sanjay Gandhi National Park

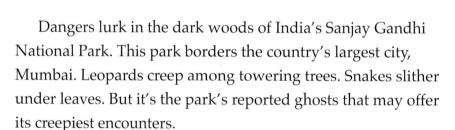

LOCATION: MUMBAI, INDIA

Dangers lurk in the dark woods of India's Sanjay Gandhi National Park. This park borders the country's largest city, Mumbai. Leopards creep among towering trees. Snakes slither under leaves. But it's the park's reported ghosts that may offer its creepiest encounters.

Wildlife in the park have taken the lives of dozens of people. Some people believe the spirits of these victims wander the park. The park's most commonly seen ghost is a female dressed in white. She is hitchhiking. At night she stands beside the road waiting for a car to approach. When a driver pulls over, she asks for a ride. But before getting in the car, she vanishes.

Park visitors report other paranormal activity. People say they've heard voices when no one is around. They report the uncomfortable feeling of being watched. The park closes during the evening. If the stories are true, maybe it's good that visitors leave before darkness settles.

Many Versions of the Vanishing Hitchhiker

People tell tales of vanishing ghostly hitchhikers throughout the world. No one knows how the **legends** began. Many of the stories go back hundreds of years. European stories tell of travelers riding on horseback who met lifelike ghosts wanting to join them. American stories from the 1870s tell of hitchhiking ghosts approaching travelers in carriages and wagons.

No matter the story, two parts usually stay the same. The hitchhiker is almost always female and she always vanishes suddenly. Sometimes the ghost disappears following its request for a ride, but usually it disappears during the journey. In some stories the hitchhiker leaves behind an item such as a jacket.

legend—a story passed down through the years that may not be completely true

Kellie's Castle

LOCATION: BATU GAJAH, MALAYSIA

In Batu Gajah, Malaysia, winding roads lead to an old, lonely castle at the top of a hill. Kellie's Castle is named for Scottish businessman and farmer William Kellie Smith. Smith began building the castle in the early 1900s. He wanted it to look like his previous home in Scotland. He planned for it to have unique and grand features, such as Malaysia's first elevator. But he never got the chance to finish the project. In the late 1920s Smith died suddenly. His wife left Malaysia with their children. The castle remains unfinished today. Yet it may not be completely abandoned. According to local stories, several ghosts have made it their home.

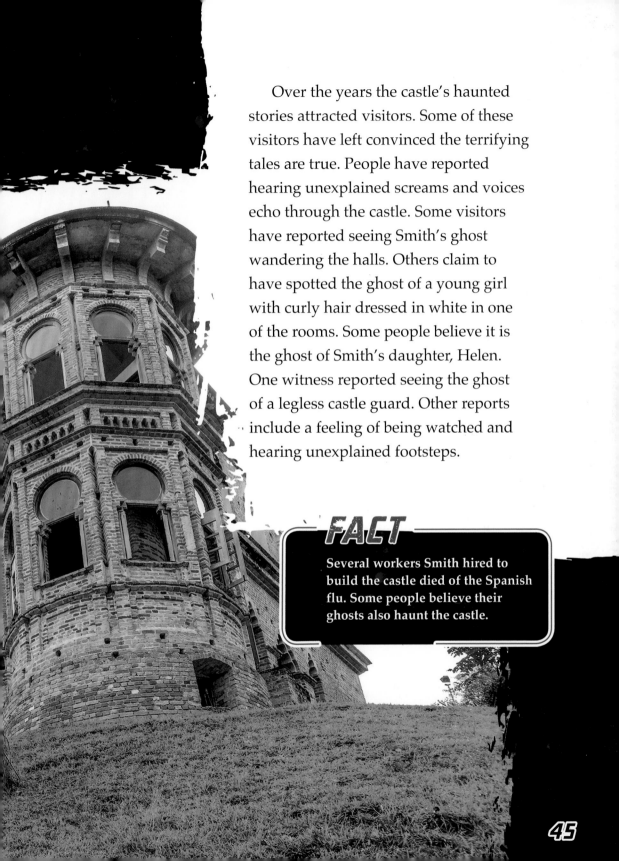

Over the years the castle's haunted stories attracted visitors. Some of these visitors have left convinced the terrifying tales are true. People have reported hearing unexplained screams and voices echo through the castle. Some visitors have reported seeing Smith's ghost wandering the halls. Others claim to have spotted the ghost of a young girl with curly hair dressed in white in one of the rooms. Some people believe it is the ghost of Smith's daughter, Helen. One witness reported seeing the ghost of a legless castle guard. Other reports include a feeling of being watched and hearing unexplained footsteps.

FACT

Several workers Smith hired to build the castle died of the Spanish flu. Some people believe their ghosts also haunt the castle.

Chaonei No. 81

LOCATION: BEIJING, CHINA

Vines creep up the sides of an empty brick mansion in Beijing, China. Oddly shaped pieces of broken glass sit in window openings. The mansion's walls inside are covered in **graffiti**. Leaves and branches litter the floor. No one has lived in the home for more than 50 years. But some locals believe the house may not really be empty.

Ownership records for Chaonei No. 81 are incomplete. Legend says that an officer fighting in the Chinese Civil War (1927–1949) once lived there. After defeat in 1949, he escaped to Taiwan. He left his wife behind. She was heartbroken and lonely. In her despair, she ended her own life. Locals claim her ghost has haunted the house ever since.

graffiti—pictures drawn or words written with spray paint on buildings, bridges, and trains; most graffiti is illegal

FACT

Chaonei No. 81 was the setting for the 2014 movie *The House That Never Dies* and its 2017 sequel. Since the first movie's release, daring thrill seekers have come to the house hoping to find out for themselves if it's haunted.

sequel—a movie or book that continues a story begun in an earlier one

People have reported many paranormal activities at the mansion. During thunderstorms loud screams are said to echo throughout the house. Some people report an uneasy feeling when passing by the home. Visitors say that the air at the front door is much cooler than it is in surrounding areas. Paranormal experts believe that large temperature drops may be a sign that ghosts are present.

The city of Beijing has the mansion on a historic building **preservation** list. This might be one of the reasons why it has remained empty for so long. It can only be fixed up, not torn down, which would be very expensive. The stories about its ghosts might keep people away too.

Stories of Mysterious Disappearances

Rumors tell of people disappearing from Chaonei No. 81. According to one story, the Chinese government built the mansion as a gift to the Catholic Church. A British priest oversaw the construction of the home around 1910. One day he suddenly went missing. Investigators later discovered a tunnel that stretched from the **crypt** in the building's basement to the nearby neighborhood of Dashanzi. The priest was never found. Did he die in the crypt? Did he escape to Dashanzi? More than 100 years later, his disappearance remains unsolved.

Another story tells of a group of construction workers who were fixing up a neighboring home's basement. Late one summer night in 2001, the men discovered a thin wall that separated the home from Chaonei No. 81. They decided to break through the wall. It's said they were never seen again.

crypt—an underground chamber

preservation—protecting something so that it stays in its
    original condition

Jeruk Purut Cemetery

LOCATION: JAKARTA, INDONESIA

Weather-beaten headstones rise from the earth. Dead bodies rest below the grass. Few places are spookier than cemeteries. Jeruk Purut Cemetery in Jakarta, Indonesia, is no exception.

Jeruk Purut's most well-known ghost is that of an old pastor. This headless figure roams the cemetery carrying his head. The ghost of a large black dog follows closely behind him. Some people believe the pastor is searching for his grave. According to legend, he appears on Friday nights only when visitors are in groups of odd-numbered people.

The headless pastor's search for his grave site may never end. It is believed his grave is actually located in Tanah Kusir Cemetery in Bintaro, South Jakarta.

A cemetery caretaker has given ghost tours at Jeruk Purut. He said one time he could not put his foot down on the ground. He claimed a child ghost kept lifting it up. He also talked of a hairy ghost that shows itself near a stream on the property.

FACT

The 2006 Indonesian horror movie *Hantu Jeruk Purut* is based on the story of the headless pastor ghost.

Penang War Museum

LOCATION: PENANG, MALAYSIA

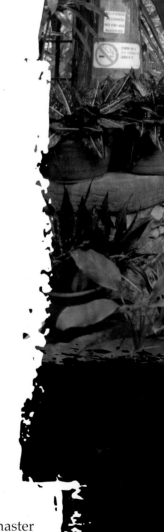

High on a hill in Penang, Malaysia, sits one of Asia's most haunted structures. The British built the fort in the 1930s. During World War II, Japanese forces overtook it. The Japanese used the fort as a prisoner-of-war camp. The fort's haunted history has earned it the name "Ghost Hill."

According to legend, a merciless leader named Tadashi Suzuki helped run the prison. He carried a **samurai** sword and used it to kill prisoners. Both prisoners and other soldiers feared him. After the war the building was empty for more than 50 years.

In 2002, the building became the Penang War Museum. Museum workers claim to have seen ghosts roaming the property. A night guard once saw a ghost holding a rifle with a bayonet in one hand. In the other hand was a samurai sword. Was it the ghost of Suzuki?

samurai—a skilled Japanese warrior who served one master or leader; the samurai fought between 500 and 1877

Today people from around the world come to the Penang War Museum. Some of these visitors are paranormal enthusiasts. Ghost hunters who have visited say they've heard the voices of ghosts. One says he even had a short conversation with a ghost. He said he asked what the ghost wanted him to do. The ghost replied, "to die."

Changi Beach

LOCATION: CHANGI, SINGAPORE

White sand stretches along the coast of Changi Beach in Singapore. By day it is a peaceful place. But by night, it might be downright terrifying.

During World War II, a horrific war crime happened at Changi Beach. Japanese forces wanted to kill all Chinese **civilians** in Singapore they believed to be anti-Japanese. On February 20, 1942, a merciless Japanese firing squad killed 66 Chinese men at the water's edge. Workers buried their bodies nearby.

FACT

After the war some Japanese soldiers found guilty of war crimes were also executed at Changi Beach.

civilian—a person who is not in the military

Today some people believe the ghosts of the killed civilians haunt the beach. Visitors have heard unexplained cries and screams. They've seen headless ghosts walking along the shore. These ghosts hold their heads in their arms. Visitors to the beach houses have reported feeling like they are being watched. They have also said that the beach house doors open and shut on their own.

The Forbidden City

LOCATION: BEIJING, CHINA

In the heart of Beijing, China, stands a palace complex known as the Forbidden City. Many betrayals and deaths have happened since it was built. Today people link these events to the paranormal experiences visitors report there.

Builders finished the Forbidden City in 1420. It was a palace for emperors. Until the early 1900s, 24 emperors ruled China from the palace. Emperor Yongle was the first to live there. He was a cruel leader, and he treated Chinese citizens poorly. In 1421, Yongle ordered his soldiers to kill thousands of people. He thought the people could reveal his secrets. Most of these victims were women.

Emperor Yongle

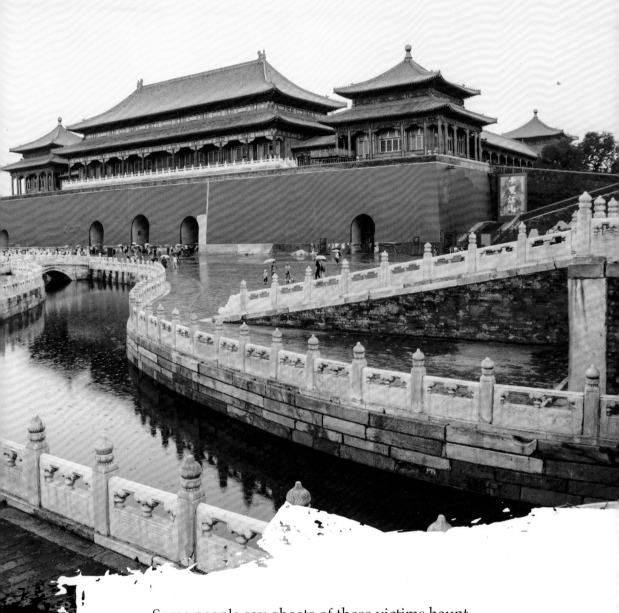

Some people say ghosts of these victims haunt the palace today. According to a soldier nicknamed Fat Fu, in 1995, two guards were on patrol. They met a woman with long hair in a black dress. They called to her, but she did not respond and ran away. They chased her. When they caught up to her, she turned to them. The men quickly saw she had no face!

Other female ghosts may haunt the palace. People say a ghostly woman dressed in white roams the grounds. She is always crying. People have also heard women's sorrowful cries at night.

Before being destroyed, the home was well known for ghost sightings. People at the base were curious about the home and sometimes explored the building's interior. Some people reported seeing the ghost of a woman washing her hair in the sink. The home's lights flickered on and off and its faucets ran and stopped for no apparent reason. Some people witnessed the ghost of a samurai riding on horseback through the home. The building is said to be across the street from a samurai's tomb.

Today many people believe the site remains haunted. A daycare center borders the land where the building once stood. Daycare workers have said that children claim to talk to other kids on the old building's site. But the daycare workers don't see any other children!

Clark Air Base Hospital

LOCATION: ANGELES, PHILIPPINES

Desperate cries call from the **morgue**. A ghost with a skeleton face wanders around the lobby. These are just a couple of the paranormal activities reported at the Clark Air Base hospital in Angeles, Philippines.

Clark Air Base was built in the early 1900s for American military forces. Its hospital saw heavy use during the Vietnam War (1959–1975). In 1991, the volcanic Mt. Pinatubo erupted and blanketed the base with 12 feet (3.7 meters) of ash. Afterward, the Americans chose to leave.

After its abandonment, people began spreading tales of ghostly events at the hospital. Some people said ghosts threw objects at them. A former property guard said he heard shouts coming from the hospital's morgue. "Help me, help me. I don't want to die," the voices said.

In 2009, team members of Ghost Hunters International visited the site. They heard unexplained footsteps. One person saw a white figure that quickly vanished. Could it have been the ghost of a fallen soldier?

morgue—a place where dead bodies are kept

Haunted Locations of Asia

1. Z High Street · Hong Kong, China

2. Sanjay Gandhi National Park · Mumbai, India

3. Kellie's Castle · Batu Gajah, Malaysia

4. Chaonei No. 81 · Beijing, China

5. Jeruk Purut Cemetery · Jakarta, Indonesia

6. Penang War Museum · Penang, Malaysia

7. Changi Beach, Changi, Singapore

8. The Forbidden City · Beijing, China

9. Building ZZ83, Kadena Air Base · Okinawa, Japan

10. Clark Air Base Hospital · Angeles, Philippines

11. Tat Tak School · Hong Kong, China

12. Bhangarh Fort · Rajasthan, India

13. Haunted House of Jeddah · Jeddah, Saudi Arabia

14. Al Qasimi Palace · Ras Al Khaimah,
    United Arab Emirates

Famous Ghost Stories of North America

TABLE OF CONTENTS

Spooky Sights in North America

People tell spooky ghost stories in every corner of the world. Stories about North America's haunted places are just as varied as the continent's landscape. Are armed ghosts fighting military battles that ended hundreds of years ago? Do ghosts of children haunt a Mexican museum filled with mummies? Could the headless ghost of a train conductor be looking for his head in Canada's countryside? Explore some of the scariest ghost tales of North America and decide for yourself.

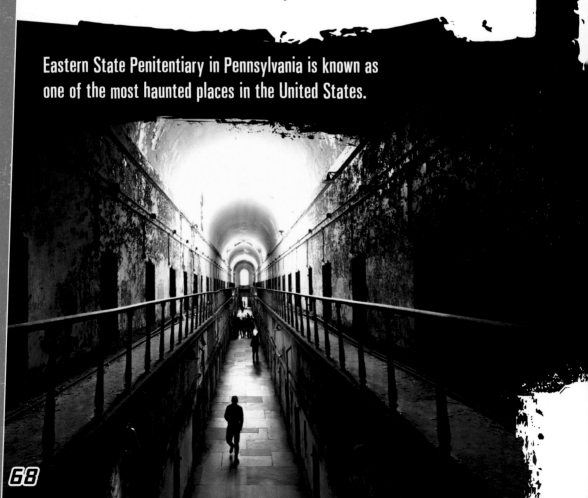

Eastern State Penitentiary in Pennsylvania is known as one of the most haunted places in the United States.

Waverly Hills Sanatorium

LOCATION: LOUISVILLE, KENTUCKY

In 1910, a small hospital opened in Louisville, Kentucky, to treat people suffering from **tuberculosis**. Back then there was no cure for the disease. As the disease spread, a larger hospital opened on the site called Waverly Hills Sanatorium. Before Waverly Hills closed in 1961, as many as 6,000 people had died there. Today it is said to be one of the most haunted places in the United States.

FACT

The doctors at Waverly Hills didn't want patients to see the dead bodies being carried out. Workers built a tunnel to move the bodies out of the hospital. The tunnel became known as the "Death Chute."

tuberculosis—a disease caused by bacteria that causes fever, weight loss, and coughing; left untreated, tuberculosis can lead to death

The ghost of a young boy named Timmy is one of the most famous ghosts at Waverly Hills. When Timmy was a patient at Waverly, it's said he loved to play with a leather ball. After hearing this story, hospital visitors began bringing brightly colored balls for him. Some visitors say they have placed balls on the ground and asked Timmy to play. The balls then rolled across the floor without being touched.

People have reported seeing the ghosts of former patients throughout the hospital. They include the ghost of an elderly woman who roams the hospital bleeding from her chained hands and feet. A dark shadowy ghost called the Creeper is said to bring a feeling of doom to anyone who is nearby.

Room 502 is considered one of the most haunted places in the hospital. Stories say a nurse took her own life there. People have reported seeing a ghostly uniformed nurse in the room. Some witnesses said she told them to get out. In 2010, a team of ghost hunters investigated the hospital for their TV show. They claim to have recorded ghostly voices in the room.

FACT

Many people have reported smelling food cooking in the kitchen at Waverly Hills. But the kitchen has been shut down for years!

Waverly Hills has been empty since 1981. But it remains a popular attraction for ghost hunters and other tourists.

Fairmont Hotel

LOCATION: VANCOUVER,
BRITISH COLUMBIA, CANADA

From the outside, the Fairmont Hotel appears to be just another luxury hotel in Vancouver. But it may not be as commonplace as it seems. Some visitors have left the building convinced it's haunted.

The most famous ghost story tells of a woman named Jennie Pearl Cox. She often visited the Fairmont Hotel to attend social events in the early 1940s. Cox was killed in a car accident in front of the hotel. Since then, visitors have reported seeing the ghost of a beautiful woman dressed in a red gown wandering the hotel. The ghost often walks through elevator doors. The "Lady in Red" stays mostly on the 14th floor. Some 14th-floor guests have said the Lady in Red was in their rooms.

In 2017, a man snapped a photo he said proved the Lady in Red was haunting the Fairmont. The image appears to show a figure in red staring out a 14th-floor window. When the photo was taken, the 14th floor was closed to guests while repairs were being made. **Skeptics** say it might have been a red tarp or other piece of material that repair workers placed there.

skeptic—a person who questions things that other people believe in

Island of the Dolls

For many children, dolls are a source of happiness and comfort. But quite the opposite is true if the dolls are eyeless, limbless objects filled with evil spirits. A small island near Mexico City is said to be haunted by the ghost of a young girl who drowned nearby. According to a legend, Julian Santana Barrera found the girl dead in the water. He also found a doll floating in the water near her body. He hung the doll from a nearby tree to honor the young girl. But he soon heard unexplained screams and footsteps. He believed the ghost of the girl haunted the area. He then began to collect hundreds of dolls, hanging them from trees all over the island. He believed they would make her ghost happy. Today more than 1,000 dolls fill the island. Many of them are falling apart and have missing eyes or limbs. Their ragged appearance only adds to the creepiness of the island.

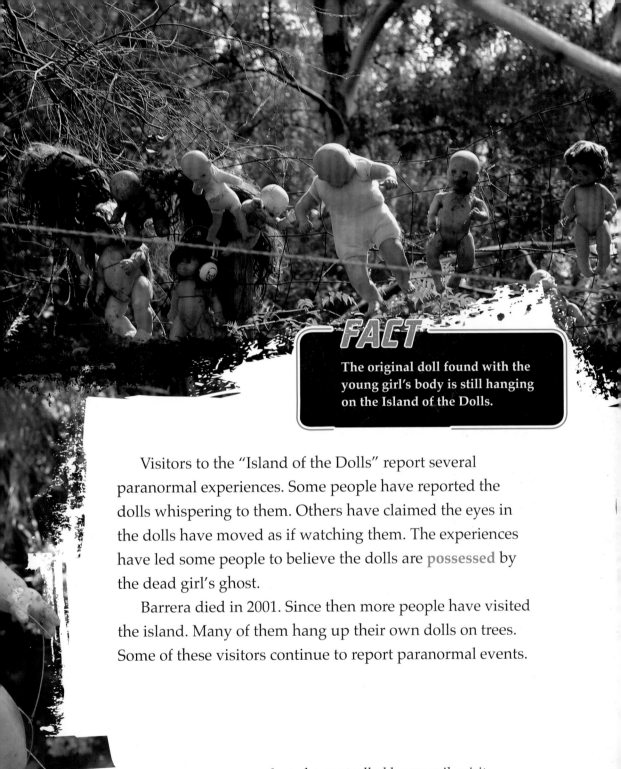

FACT

The original doll found with the young girl's body is still hanging on the Island of the Dolls.

Visitors to the "Island of the Dolls" report several paranormal experiences. Some people have reported the dolls whispering to them. Others have claimed the eyes in the dolls have moved as if watching them. The experiences have led some people to believe the dolls are **possessed** by the dead girl's ghost.

Barrera died in 2001. Since then more people have visited the island. Many of them hang up their own dolls on trees. Some of these visitors continue to report paranormal events.

possessed—to be controlled by an evil spirit

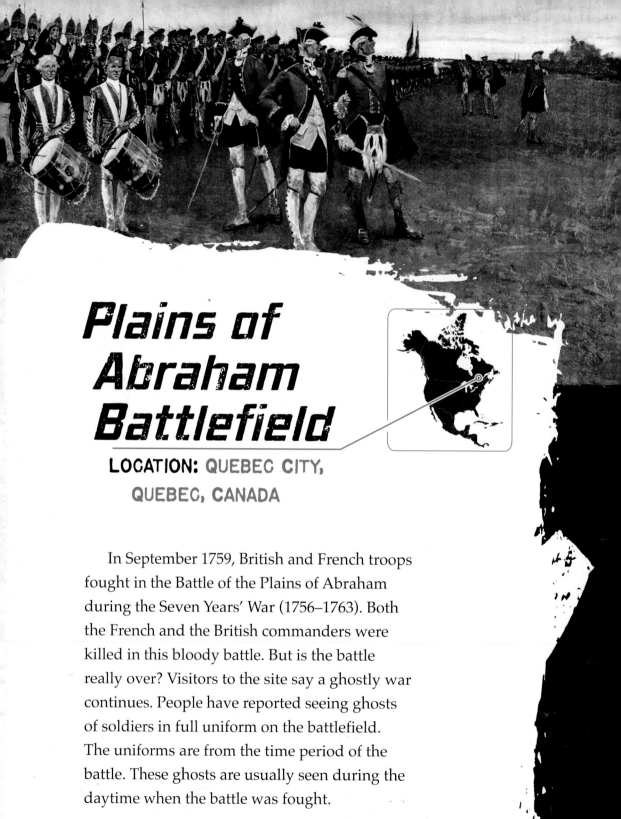

Plains of Abraham Battlefield

LOCATION: QUEBEC CITY, QUEBEC, CANADA

In September 1759, British and French troops fought in the Battle of the Plains of Abraham during the Seven Years' War (1756–1763). Both the French and the British commanders were killed in this bloody battle. But is the battle really over? Visitors to the site say a ghostly war continues. People have reported seeing ghosts of soldiers in full uniform on the battlefield. The uniforms are from the time period of the battle. These ghosts are usually seen during the daytime when the battle was fought.

A series of tunnels is near the old battlefield. Many people have reported ghostly encounters near the tunnel entrances. These reports include being touched by unseen forces. Many people have reported the smell of sulfur from cannons being fired. Both the British and French used cannons in the Battle of the Plains of Abraham.

Do the Dead Soldier On?

Soldiers are trained to never give up in battle. Ghost hunters say that is why people report so many ghostly encounters at former battlefields. The soldiers may not be able to give up the fight, even in death. During the American Civil War (1861-1865), the Battle of Gettysburg claimed the lives of about 7,000 Americans. One bloody battle of the Mexican-American War (1846-1848) happened in 1846 in San Pasqual, California. Witnesses have reported ghost sightings where these battles were fought. Reports include bloody ghost soldiers and ghostly figures of dead soldiers lying on the former battlefields.

Portland Tunnels

LOCATION: PORTLAND, OREGON

Portland, Oregon, is one of the largest cities in the Pacific Northwest. It may also be one of the most haunted cities in the United States. Many reported hauntings involve a series of tunnels running under the streets of downtown Portland. In the late 1800s, workers used the tunnels to move supplies between ships and local businesses. The tunnels also had an evil use known as shanghaiing. Criminals drugged customers in the local saloons and forced them through trapdoors into the tunnels. They sometimes took the victims to the nearby shipping ports and sold them as slaves to ship captains. Hundreds of people died in the tunnels after being kidnapped. Locals say the ghosts of these victims haunt the tunnels today.

shanghai—to kidnap and put someone aboard a ship by force

A woman named Nina is said to be one of the ghosts. According to legend, she was thrown down an elevator shaft at the Merchant Hotel. Today the hotel is a pizza shop. Nina's ghost is said to be a regular guest there. People say they've also seen her in the tunnels under the shop. She usually wears a long, black dress. Some people have reported smelling her perfume as she floated past them. Others say she tugged on their clothing.

One pizza shop worker reported a scary encounter with Nina. He said he heard a noise behind him. When he turned, he saw the ghostly form of a woman in black moving toward him. The ghost looked at him and floated toward the tunnel.

A ghost hunter investigates the tunnels under downtown Portland.

The Mummy Museum

LOCATION: GUANAJUATO CITY, GUANAJUATO, MEXICO

In the late 1860s, people of Guanajuato, Mexico, paid a fee to have their dead relatives placed in the city cemetery. They had to continue to pay money to keep them there. If they could no longer pay, their relative was removed from the cemetery crypts. When cemetery workers removed bodies, they often found the remains in excellent condition. The dry **climate** and lack of air in the crypts naturally turned the bodies into **mummies**. For many years workers placed the mummified remains into a storage building. In the 1950s, the city built the Guanajuato Mummy Museum to display the remains.

climate—the usual weather that occurs in a place

mummy—a body that has been preserved

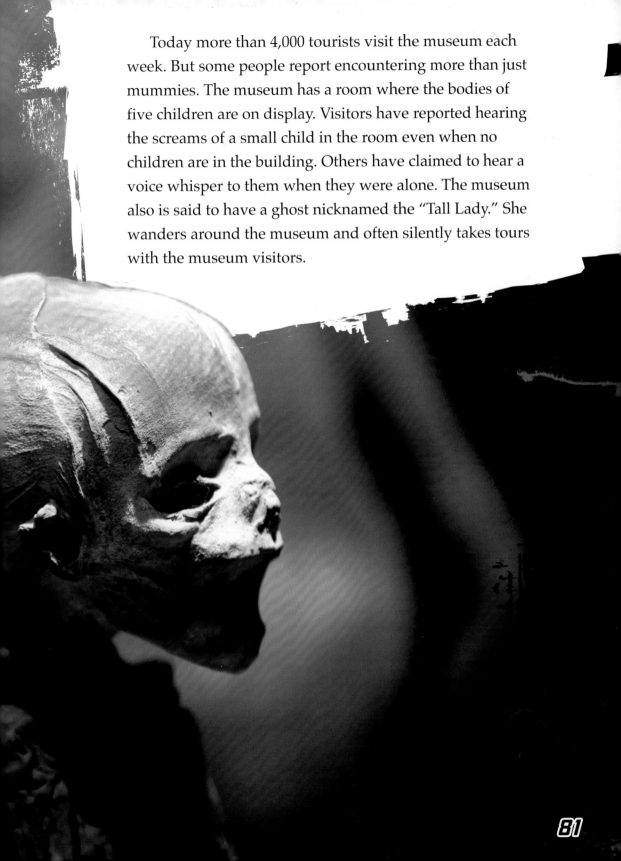

Today more than 4,000 tourists visit the museum each week. But some people report encountering more than just mummies. The museum has a room where the bodies of five children are on display. Visitors have reported hearing the screams of a small child in the room even when no children are in the building. Others have claimed to hear a voice whisper to them when they were alone. The museum also is said to have a ghost nicknamed the "Tall Lady." She wanders around the museum and often silently takes tours with the museum visitors.

Many islands of the Isles of Shoals have rocky coasts.

Isles of Shoals

LOCATION: NEAR THE
U.S. EASTERN COAST

Nine small islands off the coast of Maine and New Hampshire are the setting of several ghost stories. People have reported paranormal activity on the Isles of Shoals for hundreds of years. Some well-known pirates used the islands as stopping points. According to one legend, the famous pirate known as Blackbeard once left his wife behind on Lunging Island to guard his treasure. But he never returned, and she died. Visitors to the island have reported seeing her pale white ghost. The ghost is said to whisper, "He will return."

A shipwreck in 1813 on Smuttynose Island led to one of its ghostly tales. The ship crashed into the island during a winter storm. Fourteen Spanish soldiers plunged into the icy waters of the Atlantic Ocean. According to local stories, the wet, freezing men tried to crawl to the only house on the island. Tragically, they didn't make it. When the island's caretaker came out the next morning, he found their bodies frozen in the snow. Two men almost made it to the house, dying near the wall outside the property.

Today visitors to Smuttynose Island report chilling encounters with the dead sailors. Witnesses say the ghostly men wander the island as though they are searching for their ship to return home. The ship itself is even said to make ghostly appearances near Smuttynose.

Brockamour Manor

LOCATION: NIAGARA-ON-THE-LAKE, ONTARIO, CANADA

A cozy hotel called Brockamour Manor lies in the small town of Niagara-on-the-Lake in Ontario, Canada. But are its charming surroundings hiding a spooky secret?

Lady Sophia Shaw lived in the home that is now Brockamour in 1812. She was in love with Canadian Army General Isaac Brock. The two planned to marry when the War of 1812 ended. However, General Brock was killed in battle. Lady Sophia was heartbroken. She lived for a few more years in the home, but it's said she was never seen again in public. She locked herself away on the second floor. She died alone in the home in 1814. But she may have never left. For more than 200 years, witnesses have reported seeing her ghost at the Brockamour. She often appears on the second floor. Guests also claim to hear her uncontrollable crying late at night.

Locals also have reported seeing Lady Sophia's ghost throughout Niagara-on-the-Lake. They have spotted her walking along Queen Street crying. Locals have nicknamed the ghost "Sobbing Sophia."

FACT

A monument stands in Niagara-on-the-Lake to honor the life of General Brock. Witnesses have claimed to see the General's ghost in full military dress alongside his statue.

The St. Louis Ghost Train

LOCATION: ST. LOUIS, SASKATCHEWAN, CANADA

According to locals in St. Louis, Saskatchewan, Canada, a deadly train accident led to an eerie haunting north of town. According to the story, a conductor was working one night in the 1920s when a train ran over him. His head was cut off in the accident. Since then people have reported a ghostly light in the area. Witnesses say the unexplained light looks like the headlight of a train coming down the tracks. Locals call the light the "St. Louis Ghost Train" or the "St. Louis Light." The light is usually a white haze. Some reports say the light fades and grows brighter as it moves. Some people report seeing a red light with the white light. Legend says the red light is the lantern the headless conductor carries as he searches for his head. The city has removed the train tracks, yet the ghostly sightings continue.

Not everyone believes the lights are paranormal. Some skeptics say headlights reflecting from passing cars cause the strange light. Other people say swamp gas is responsible. Some people believe that as methane gas from swamps rises, it can mix with other gases. The mixture causes glowing lights.

In 2014 Canada made a postage stamp with a train on it to honor the famous legend of the St Louis Ghost Train. It was part of a series showing famous Canadian ghost stories.

El Hotel Meson de Jobito

LOCATION: ZACATECAS CITY, ZACATECAS, MEXICO

Some visitors to the popular El Hotel Meson de Jobito have left with a terrifying memory of their visit. Guests regularly report hearing the sound of children jumping and shouting when there are no children nearby. Some people report objects being moved mysteriously or feelings of being watched. Visitors report most of the paranormal activity at about 4:00 a.m.

Most reports involve unexplained noises. Guests have said they've been awakened by the sound of horses running through the halls. When workers investigate they can't find anything to explain the sound.

Ghost hunters often request to stay in room 107. People report the most paranormal activity there. The room is said to have belonged to a caretaker of the hotel named Don Jobito.

Alcatraz Prison

LOCATION: ALCATRAZ ISLAND, CALIFORNIA

Alcatraz Prison in San Francisco Bay, California, is a former federal prison. The U.S. government now operates it as a tourist attraction. Opened in 1934, it was once home to some of the most dangerous criminals in the United States. **Riots** and fights at Alcatraz left dozens of prisoners dead. Others died while trying to escape the island prison. Workers moved the last prisoner off of "The Rock" more than 50 years ago. However, visitors to the island say plenty of them stayed behind to haunt their former home.

riot—a large gathering of people who use violence to show their anger

Chicago gangster Al Capone is one of the most commonly reported Alcatraz ghosts. Capone passed time in the prison playing the banjo. Dozens of prison visitors have reported the sound of a banjo being played in his former cell. Tourists say they've felt bursts of cold air while approaching the cell. Unexplained temperature drops are said to be a sign that ghosts are nearby.

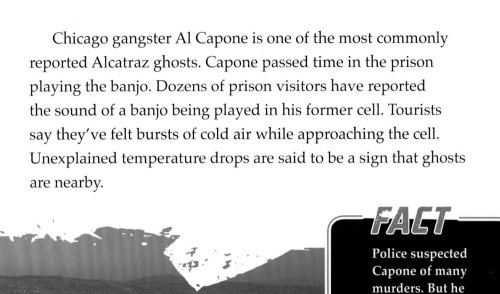

FACT

Police suspected Capone of many murders. But he was jailed for not paying taxes.

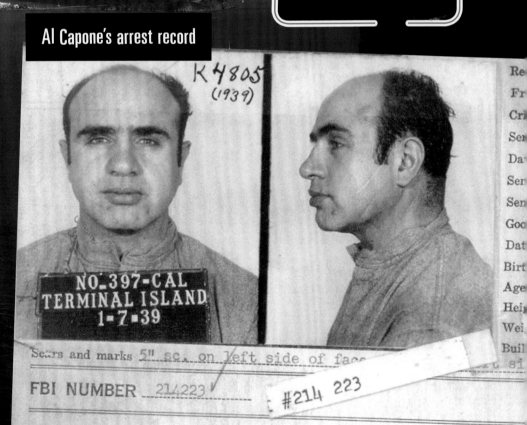

Al Capone's arrest record

K4805
(1939)

Re
Fr
Cri
Ser
Da
Ser
Sen
Goo
Dat
Birt
Age
Hei
Wei
Buil
s

NO. 397-CAL
TERMINAL ISLAND
1-7-39

Scars and marks 5" sc. on left side of face

FBI NUMBER 214/223

#214 223

CRIMINAL HISTORY

| NAME | NUMBER | CITY OR INSTITUTION | |

More Than Prisoner Ghosts

It may not be just prisoners who haunt Alcatraz. Before European settlers arrived in North America, American Indians sometimes used the island to punish tribe members. They believed evil spirits lived on the island. Perhaps these spirits are responsible for some the island's paranormal events.

Cell Block D is said to be one of the most haunted areas of the prison. Prisoners were often sent to Block D after breaking prison rules. Prisoner Rufus McCain was often moved to cell 14D. Another prisoner killed McCain in 1940. A prisoner being held in the cell after McCain's death claimed that an unseen monster with red eyes was trying to kill him. Guards found the prisoner dead in the morning. He had been strangled. The murder was never solved. Some people believe the ghost of McCain killed him. Today visitors have reported that cell 14D is unusually cold. Visitors to Block D also often report hearing unexplained voices.

Haunted Locations of North America

1. **Waverly Hills Sanatorium,** Louisville, Kentucky

2. **Fairmont Hotel, Vancouver,** British Columbia, Canada

3. **Island of the Dolls,** Mexico City, Mexico

4. **Plains of Abraham Battlefield,** Quebec City, Quebec, Canada

5. **Portland Tunnels, Portland, Oregon**

6. **The Mummy Museum, Guanajuato City,** Guanajuato, Mexico

7. **Isles of Shoals, off the coast** of Maine and New Hampshire

8. **Brockamour Manor,** Niagara-on-the-Lake, Ontario, Canada

9. **The St. Louis Ghost Train, St. Louis,** Saskatchewan, Canada

10. **El Hotel Meson de Jobito, Zacatecas City,** Zacatecas, Mexico

11. **Alcatraz Prison, San Francisco Bay, California**

12. **Myrtles Plantation, St. Francisville, Louisiana**

13. **Eastern State Penitentiary, Philadelphia, Pennsylvania**

14. **Silent Zone, Durango, Mexico**

15. **Sanatorio Duran, Provincia de Cartago, Costa Rica**

16. **Xunantunich Ruins, San Jose Succotz, Belize**

17. **Rose Hall, Montego Bay, Jamaica**

FAMOUS GHOST STORIES OF EUROPE

TABLE OF CONTENTS

Are You Scared Yet?

What's the scariest ghost story you've ever heard? Maybe it was a tale about a local house or hotel. People tell stories about creepy haunted places around the world. Some of the world's most terrifying ghost stories are from Europe. People have reported seeing headless ghosts haunting old castles. Hotel guests say they've been touched by spirits from beyond the grave. These ghostly encounters often happen in places where many people have died. Are the ghost stories fact or fiction? Decide for yourself after you explore some of the most well-known haunted places in Europe.

Thinking about visiting the Paris Catacombs in France?

You might change your mind after learning about their reported hauntings!

Ancient Ram Inn

LOCATION: GLOUCESTERSHIRE, ENGLAND

The Ancient Ram Inn is said to be one of the most haunted inns in England. The ghost of Mary Gibbons is especially well known there. In the 1500s, witch hunts became common in Europe. Locals sometimes tied suspected witches to stakes and burned them to death. Gibbons had been accused of being a witch. She tried to hide at the inn, but she was found and put to death.

Today Gibbons' ghost is said to haunt the "Witch's Room." People have reported seeing dark shapes moving in the room. Ghost hunters have claimed to hear the voice of Mary's ghost there. They say her spirit was heard on tape answering questions.

For decades the inn has been a private residence, but that hasn't stopped the creepy reports from coming. Owner John Humphries claims to have regular run-ins with the dead. Humphries told a tale of being dragged from his bed by what he called a demon force on his first night in the home.

Visitors to the inn continue to report unexplained experiences. Ghost hunters say they've captured the voice of a male ghost using **EVP** equipment. People have reported **orbs** in photographs they took at the inn. Paranormal experts believe orbs could be a sign that ghosts were present when a photo was taken.

EVP—sounds or voices heard during electronic recordings that can't be explained; EVP stands for electronic voice phenomenon

orb—a glowing ball of light that sometimes appears in photographs taken at reportedly haunted locations

Why are all these creepy happenings being reported at the inn? Some paranormal experts say a ley line is to blame. A ley line is said to form when two landforms or structures are connected by a straight line. Some people believe these lines allow energy and ghosts to travel freely between the two places. The inn sits on the intersection of two ley lines connecting it to Stonehenge. Stonehenge is one of the most famous tourist attractions in England. The stone structure and its burial ground date back more than 5,000 years. Could the spirits of those buried at Stonehenge be traveling the ley line to the Ancient Ram Inn?

Wolfsegg Castle

LOCATION: WOLFSEGG, GERMANY

Wolfsegg, Germany, is home to an 800-year-old castle with a mysterious past. For many years visitors have reported encounters with a spirit known as the "Woman in White." Many people think the ghost is the spirit of Klara von Helfenstein. She was murdered in the castle in the 1500s.

Some of the creepiest reports don't even include ghost sightings. Visitors have reported feeling unexplained sadness near the room where Klara died. They also have reported feeling pulled to the room by an invisible force.

The Woman in White may be spooky, but locals say the true terror of Wolfsegg is found in the dark woods behind the castle. Daring visitors who go there can find The Hole. Locals say this cave holds many dark secrets. For hundreds of years, people have reported strange, terrifying noises coming from inside. Moaning and wailing sounds are said to pierce the night, shattering the silence of the forest.

A legend says the terror of The Hole dates back to the disappearance of a man named Georg Moller. Klara von Helfenstein had hired Moller for protection while her husband was away. Soon after Klara was murdered, he went walking in the woods behind the castle. He was never seen again. Locals say that since then, others who have dared to go exploring in the woods have also vanished.

FACT

Some people say the two men who murdered Klara von Helfenstein also haunt the castle.

In the 1920s, scientists went into The Hole to try to find out more about what was happening there. They found hundreds of animal bones. Are animals making the wails and moans coming from the darkness or is something far creepier responsible?

Raynham Hall

LOCATION: NORFOLK, ENGLAND

Raynham Hall is said to be haunted by the ghost of a woman who has been dead for nearly 300 years. Lady Dorothy Walpole lived there with her husband, Charles Townshend, in the early 1700s. Townshend became angry with her and locked her away in a tower on the property. Unable to escape, she died sick and alone. More than 100 years after her death, a witness first reported seeing her ghost. It was the first of many reports.

Witnesses say the ghost of Lady Dorothy Walpole floats through the halls of the estate. The ghost has earned the nickname "The Brown Lady" because she is always wearing a long, brown dress. Some people say the spooky spirit has a glowing face but empty sockets where her eyes should be. Witnesses have described her as having a crazed smile on her face. Sometimes she carries a lantern.

In 1936, a photographer working for *Country Life* magazine was at Raynham Hall taking pictures. On the grand staircase, he photographed what he believed was the ghost of Lady Walpole. The magazine published the image. Soon thousands of visitors came to the estate hoping to meet its most famous ghost.

FACT

Experts have proven many of the "ghosts" in photographs to be shadows. Reflections on the lens or other lighting in a room can cause these mysterious shadows.

estate—a large area of land, usually with a house on it

Akershus Fortress

LOCATION: OSLO, NORWAY

Like many haunted places, Akershus Fortress has a violent past. King Hakon V ordered the castle built in 1299. It overlooked the Oslo Fjord. Its position allowed the military to see enemies coming toward Oslo across the water. It later was a military fortress and a prison. Prison authorities sometimes beat and killed prisoners there. Nazis later used the site during World War II (1939-1945) to carry out enemy **executions**. With so much death and misery at Akershus comes many spooky tales.

execution—putting someone to death

The ghost of a woman named Mantelgeisten reportedly lives in the fortress. Visitors have reported seeing her dressed in a long, flowing robe. Many witnesses say she has no face.

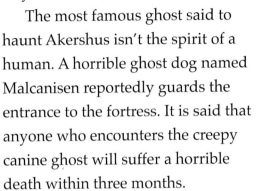

The most famous ghost said to haunt Akershus isn't the spirit of a human. A horrible ghost dog named Malcanisen reportedly guards the entrance to the fortress. It is said that anyone who encounters the creepy canine ghost will suffer a horrible death within three months.

According to legend, a commander of the Norwegian Armed Forces ordered that a dog be buried alive at the fortress's front gates hundreds of years ago. The commander believed the ghost of the dog would provide protection for the men inside. He may have been right. Over the years, military forces have attacked Akershus many times, but it was never captured by force.

FACT

In English *Malcanisen* **means "evil dog."**

Poveglia Island

LOCATION: ITALY

In the mid-1300s, a terrible disease known as the Black Death struck Europe. The disease killed about one-third of Europe's population. Many cities used islands and other isolated places to **quarantine** the sick. Poveglia Island near Venice, Italy, was home to thousands of sick Italians. Most died slow, painful deaths. Workers also transported tens of thousands of dead bodies to the island while the plague was spreading. It's said that half of the island contains human remains. It may come as no surprise that the island has long been the site of ghostly occurrences.

quarantine—to keep a person, animal, or plant away from others to stop a disease from spreading

The Italian government owned Poveglia Island until 2014. Before selling it, the government forbid visitors to go there. But brave souls still snuck onto the island to try to meet the spirits of the dead.

One of the most mysterious ghostly tales involves an old bell tower on the island. In the late 1800s, a psychiatric hospital was on the island. Legend says one doctor was known for conducting many cruel experiments on the patients. He threw himself to his death from the bell tower. Today locals living on the mainland claim to hear the bell chime. There's just one problem—the bell is no longer there! Many locals are convinced it is the dead man ringing the bell from beyond the grave.

One local Italian man reports spending 15 nights on the island in the mid-1900s. He reported seeing the ghost of a doctor. The man claims the doctor pushed him and that the ghost could make objects fly around him.

Langham Hotel

LOCATION: LONDON, ENGLAND

Sometimes ghosts in hotels seem to bother guests in certain rooms. This is true of London's Langham Hotel. If ghost hunters visit the hotel, they often request to stay in room 333. Witnesses have reported several ghosts in the room, including a doctor with blank eyes. The doctor is said to have killed his wife and himself in the room while on their honeymoon. Visitors also have reported seeing the ghost of a German prince dressed in his military uniform. The noble ghost passes through solid walls and doors. The prince is believed to have jumped to his death from an upper floor of the hotel.

In 1973, a guest staying in room 333 reported a terrifying encounter with a white orb. The ball of light transformed into a ghostly man wearing Victorian clothing right in front of his eyes! The guest fled the room in terror. The ghost has been seen several times since.

One woman staying in room 333 said a ghost had violently shook her bed. She fled the hotel in the middle of the night.

Despite these spine-tingling tales, Room 333 has become a popular tourist attraction. Ghost hunters may pay more than $650 to spend the night.

Tower of London

LOCATION: LONDON, ENGLAND

The Tower of London is more than 1,000 years old. It has a bloody history. Many people have been murdered there. One of the most mysterious tales of murder involves two young princes. In 1674, workers tearing down an old staircase in the tower uncovered two small skeletons. Nearly 200 years earlier, two young princes were killed on the grounds. Historians believe the skeletons unearthed were those of the young boys.

Today the mystery of who killed the boys and why remains. Many people suspect the boys' uncle Richard had them killed to have a better chance at becoming king.

King Charles II ordered a royal burial of the bodies at Westminster Abbey to honor them. But although the remains of the bodies are now gone, their spirits may have stayed in the tower. Many witnesses have reported seeing ghosts of the princes over the years. They are dressed in white and often hold hands, as if trying to protect each other.

The wife of one of the tower's guards once saw the ghosts dressed in white nightshirts. They held each other in front of a fireplace. When the woman told her husband, he laughed. He pointed out there was no fireplace in the room. Little did he know that behind the wall was a fireplace that had been covered up!

The Tower of London has also been the site of more than 100 executions. Visitors have reported seeing headless ghosts roaming throughout the tower since the 1300s. The most famous is the spirit of Queen Anne Boleyn, wife of King Henry VIII. She was killed in the tower in 1536. Many people have spotted her ghost wandering the grounds in a bloody dress. Witnesses often see her near the Queen's House.

Queen Anne Boleyn

Yet the dead that are said to haunt the Tower of London aren't limited to human form. One story says a guard was on patrol in 1815 when he saw smoke coming from Martin Tower. The smoky mist soon took the form of an enormous bear. The guard tried to stab the animal with his bayonet. His weapon passed right through the bear and stuck in the door. After reporting the event, the guard went into shock. He never recovered and died two days later.

Edinburgh Castle

LOCATION:

EDINBURGH, SCOTLAND

Many people consider Edinburgh Castle one of the most haunted places in Scotland. Witnesses have reported many ghostly encounters in the castle's maze of underground tunnels. Those who dare to go in them may meet up with a ghost playing the bagpipes. Legend says the man was sent to explore the underground tunnels after they were first discovered. The man brought his bagpipes and played them as he walked so that the people above could track his movement. Suddenly, the music stopped and there was silence. Those in the castle quickly formed a search party and went after the piper. But they never found him, his body, or his bagpipes.

In 2001, a team of researchers sent almost 250 people into the castle without telling them any of its haunted history. Many people reported paranormal events. Most of the reports came from areas with a history of hauntings.

If a musical ghost isn't scary enough, castle visitors have reported many other frightening experiences. People have reported seeing ghosts of soldiers. Some were said to make physical contact with the terrified witnesses. One visitor reported being touched on the face by an unseen hand. Others have felt a tugging on their clothes from behind. When they quickly turned around, there was no one there—at least no one living!

Haunted Harmonies

Do you love music? Ghosts might too. People have reported ghosts playing pianos in hotels, banjos in prisons, and drums in castles. Why? Some people believe the answer is very simple. Music makes people happy. You might dance, sing, and smile when you hear a favorite song. Maybe the spirits of the dead seek out the things that made them happy in life, including music.

The Paris Catacombs

LOCATION: PARIS, FRANCE

Paris is known as the City of Love. Many couples travel to Paris on their honeymoons or for other special occasions. But as couples stroll the streets, the bones of 6 million people lie underneath them!

In the late 1700s, people in Paris were running out of room to bury their dead. The government decided to move millions of bodies underground into a series of tunnels called catacombs. With all of these bones under Paris, it may come as no surprise that the Paris Catacombs are legendary for ghost stories.

catacomb—an underground cemetery, usually with tunnels and rooms

People have reported seeing ghosts and experiencing unexplained changes in temperature in the tunnels for many years. Some people think extreme temperature changes are a sign of ghost activity. Witnesses have claimed the skulls lining the walls came to life, moving as if watching them. Other tourists have reported hearing soft voices calling out to them from the walls of bones. Even with terrifying tales such as these, the Paris Catacombs remain a popular tourist attraction.

Ghostly Tourists

The Paris Catacombs cover nearly 200 miles (322 km) underground. Many visitors have gotten lost in these dark, winding tunnels. Deaths are rare in the catacombs. But when they do occur, they tend to get a lot of attention. The most famous disappearance involves Frenchman Philibert Aspairt. He went into the catacombs in 1793 and never returned. Visitors found his remains in 1804 near one of the exits. He appeared to have almost made it out of the deadly maze. Could his be among the spirits that haunt the passageways today?

A LA MEMOIRE
DE PHILIBERT ASPAIRT
PERDU DANS CETTE
CARRIÈRE LE III NOV.
MDCCXCIII, RETROUVÉ
ONZE ANS APRÈS ET
INHUMÉ EN LA MÈME PLACE
LE XXX AVRIL MDCCCIV

Ruthin Castle Hotel

LOCATION: RUTHIN, WALES

Paranormal researchers say ghosts often haunt the places where they died. That might explain the many reported sightings of "The Grey Lady" at Ruthin Castle Hotel. Legend says she is the ghost of a woman who was sentenced to death there. Castle workers buried her on the property hundreds of years ago.

Today the castle is a luxury hotel. Visitors who have seen the Grey Lady say she is dressed completely in gray. She floats quietly throughout the castle and outside. Many tourists claim to have captured photographs of the mysterious spirit.

FACT

The Grey Lady was buried just outside the entrance to the castle. Her grave is still visible today.

The Grey Lady isn't the only ghost reported at Ruthin Castle. People have reported sightings of a ghostly knight in full armor as well as the ghost of a small child. Some of these ghosts may even be able to interact with the living. People have reported being touched, grabbed, or even held down by unseen forces.

Haunted Places of Europe

1. **Ancient Ram Inn** · **Gloucestershire, England**
2. **Wolfsegg Castle** · **Wolfsegg, Germany**
3. **Raynham Hall** · **Norfolk, England**
4. **Akershus Fortress** · **Oslo, Norway**
5. **Poveglia Island** · **Venetian Lagoon, Italy**
6. **Langham Hotel** · **London, England**
7. **Tower of London** · **London, England**
8. **Edinburgh Castle** · **Edinburgh, Scotland**
9. **Paris Catacombs** · **Paris, France**
10. **Ruthin Castle Hotel** · **Ruthin, Wales**
11. **Leap Castle** · **County Offaly, Ireland**
12. **Houska Castle** · **Blatce, Czech Republic**
13. **The Kremlin** · **Moscow, Russia**
14. **Banffy Castle** · **Bontida, Romania**
15. **Witches' Pond** · **Boldu-Creteasca Forest, Romania**
16. **The Borgvattnet Vicarage** · **Borgvattnet, Sweden**

GLOSSARY

abandoned (uh-BAN-duhnd)—deserted or no longer used

afterlife (AF-tur-life)—the life that some people believe begins after a person dies

apartheid (uh-PAR-tayt)—a former policy of racial segregation and discrimination in South Africa

catacomb (CAT-uh-kohm)—an underground cemetery, usually with tunnels and rooms

civilian (si-VIL-yuhn)—a person who is not in the military

climate (KLY-muht)—the usual weather that occurs in a place

crypt (KRIPT)—an underground chamber

estate (e-STAYT)—a large area of land, usually with a house on it

EVP—sounds or voices heard during electronic recordings that can't be explained; EVP stands for electronic voice phenomenon

execute (EK-si-kyoot)—to put to death

execution (ek-si-KYOO-shuhn)—putting someone to death

graffiti (gruh-FEE-tee)—pictures drawn or words written with spray paint on buildings, bridges, and trains; most graffiti is illegal

haunted (HAWNT-id)—having mysterious events happen often, possibly due to visits from ghosts

legend (LEJ-uhnd)—a story passed down through the years that may not be completely true

magistrate (MA-juh-strayt)—a government official who makes and enforces laws

morgue (MORG)—a place where dead bodies are kept

mummify (MUH-mih-fy)—to preserve a body with special salts and cloth to make it last for a very long time mummy (MUH-mee)—a body that has been preserved

orb (ORB)—a glowing ball of light that sometimes appears in photographs taken at reportedly haunted locations

paranormal (pair-uh-NOR-muhl)—having to do with an event that has no scientific explanation

pharaoh (FAIR-oh)—a king of ancient Egypt

poltergeist (POLE-tuhr-gyst)—a noisy ghost

possessed (puh-ZESD)—to be controlled by an evil spirit

preservation (pre-zur-VAY-shuhn)—protecting something so that it stays in its original condition

psychiatric (sy-kee-A-trik)—related to a branch of medicine that studies the mind, emotions, and behavior

quarantine (KWOR-uhn-teen)—to keep a person, animal, or plant away from others to stop a disease from spreading

riot (RYE-uht)—a large gathering of people who use violence to show their anger

samurai (SAH-muh-rye)—a skilled Japanese warrior who served one master or leader; the samurai fought between 500 and 1877

sequel (SEE-kwul)—a movie or book that continues a story begun in an earlier one

shanghai (SHANG-hy)—to kidnap and put someone aboard a ship by force

skeptic (SKEP-tik)—a person who questions things that other people believe in

spirit (SPIHR-it)—an invisible part of a being that contains thoughts and feelings; some people believe the spirit leaves the body after death

supernatural (soo-pur-NACH-ur-uhl)—something that cannot be given an ordinary explanation

tuberculosis (tu-bur-kyoo-LOH-sis)—a disease caused by bacteria that causes fever, weight loss, and coughing; left untreated, it can lead to death

INDEX